THAT STRANGE NECESSITY

*"Cherish the Past, Adorn the Present,
Construct for the Future."*
Clough Williams-Ellis

For Wendy and Carol
with our thanks.

THAT STRANGE NECESSITY
Visions of Portmeirion

Poems by JOHN ELINGER
Illustrations by PETER HONEY

SIGNAL BOOKS
Oxford

First published in 2015 by
Signal Books Limited
36 Minster Road
Oxford
OX4 1LY
www.signalbooks.co.uk

A catalogue record for this book is available
from the British Library.

ISBN 978-1-909930-30-8 Paper

Design and production: Baseline Arts Ltd
Cover design: Baseline Arts Ltd
Illustrations: Peter Honey

CONTENTS

[6]

FOREWORD

MY GRANDFATHER CLOUGH WILLIAMS-ELLIS built Portmeirion to inspire artists. He hoped that poets, novelists, playwrights, painters and musicians might find his contrived environment to be conducive to their creative instincts and that new works might emanate as a result. It is a pleasure to welcome this beautifully produced collection of poems and watercolours that brings Portmeirion to life and captures the very essence of the place. No other book on Portmeirion tells its story from a starting-point of 500 million years ago!

Clough hoped that his experiment with 'architectural good manners' would inspire future generations. His hopes have been wonderfully realised in this volume.

ROBIN LLYWELYN, *Managing Director of Portmeirion Ltd*

INTRODUCTION

I. PORTMEIRION

Like Portofino, Clough's Portmeirion's
'an almost perfect' specimen of man's
employment and adornment of what one's
tempted to call the perfect site. His plans,
evolving over fifty years, placed beauty
first – before use – though seeking both, for these,
he taught, comprise the architectural duty
of those who build amidst such rocks and trees.
Postmodernist in style, Portmeirion
embraces old and new, brickwork and stone,
Classical, Arts & Crafts, function and fun,
to form an imagery all its own.
   This 'home for fallen buildings' is a dream
   made real – *his* vision, *his* perfected scheme.

THE ARCHITECT, SIR CLOUGH WILLIAMS-ELLIS (1883–1978), bought the estate of Aber Ia in 1925 from his uncle, Sir Osmond Williams of Deudraeth Castle. Over the years that followed, he extended the site, acquiring more land – including the Gwyllt, the adjacent farm and Deudraeth Castle itself with its park and avenue. He was determined to establish his village, renamed 'Portmeirion', in a 'green belt of woods and farmland' – which he has done.

Portmeirion is located on the Traeth Bach ('small beach') estuary of the River Dwyryd near the coast of Gwynedd in North Wales. It lies almost equidistant between Portmadoc and Penrhyndeudrath on the edge of the Snowdonia National Park, in the creation of which he also played a leading role. Caernarfon, Bangor and the Isle of Anglesey lie to the north; Bala and the English Potteries to the west; Harlech and Dolgellau to the south.

Portmeirion is situated on a sheltered, low-lying site close to the water's edge; the climate is relatively mild, rather damp and often windy, as is normal for North Wales. The wettest months are October to January, but rain is never very far away. Average temperatures range from 0–7°C in winter and 10–20°C in summer. Y Gwyllt, 'the wilderness', lying to the west of the village, provides a benign environment, not just for a wide range of native plants, but also for a number of more exotic species, such as rhododendrons, azaleas, hydrangeas and camellias. There are rabbits, foxes, badgers, hedgehogs and red squirrels; and a wide variety of birds. Attempts to introduce non-native species, such as white peacocks and green lizards, have sadly failed.

The history of Portmeirion falls conveniently into four sections: the Aber Ia period, before 1925; the earlier construction period, 1925–45; the later construction period, 1945–76; and, more recently, the years of conservation following the death of the architect in 1978. Not a lot is known about the first of these: Aber Ia formed a small detail in a larger story, the formation of Britain and its western region – Wales.

The geology of North Wales was substantially created during the Palaeozoic period, some 500 million years ago, when much of the region lay below the sea level and the Snowdon range was a fiercely active volcanic island, pouring our streams of lava over a period of many millions of years. The British Isles, as we know them, began to take shape during the Pliocene period, some ten million years ago.

However, about two million years ago, the last – and great – ice-age began: the British Isles and much of northern Europe remained frozen, with occasional warmer inter-glacial episodes, until as recently as 10,000 years ago. It is tempting to speculate that the world may be coming to the end of just another inter-glacial episode at present. Such a hypothesis could perhaps explain why the forecast 'global warming' is apparently not developing as fast as was feared: a new (and natural) ice-age might be expected to suppress, or at least retard, the effects of the man-made 'greenhouse effect'. We shall see.

[9]

Co-incidentally, our species (*homo sapiens*) was evolving from earlier proto-human primates somewhere in Africa at the beginning of the ice-age, almost ten million years ago. This new (extraordinarily – and dangerously – successful) species gradually spread throughout the world and settled in every continent – except Antarctica.

Some early humans reached the southern areas of Britain during the inter-glacial periods and settled briefly, but the land was not securely populated until the ice finally receded. Since then, there has been a constant stream of immigrants, some arriving peacefully, others by conquest – Picts, Celts, Romans, Anglo-Saxons, Vikings, Norman French, gipsies, Huguenots and others – and (in our own time) citizens of the Commonwealth and Europe. We are all immigrants, or the descendants of immigrants!

The re-population of Britain began in about 8000 BC. A number of different groups settled here during the later Stone Age and the Bronze Age, of whom little is clearly known. But from about 500 BC, when the Iron Age began and the Celtic immigrants arrived, we have a reasonable historical record. It seems that the Celtic-speaking peoples conquered, and gradually settled in, the whole of the British Isles. Their language survives into modern times in Irish and Scots Gaelic, Cornish (and emigrant Breton), Manx and, of course, Welsh.

The subsequent Roman invasion, from the first century BC, and the later Anglo-Saxon invasion, from the fifth century AD, forced them to move westwards and northwards in Britain, and eradicated the Celtic language in what became England, the land of the Anglo-Saxons. Since that time, Wales – and the Welsh (which is an Old English word meaning 'strangers') – have continued to assert their independence as a nation and a culture, with no little success.

Aber Ia, 'the frozen estuary', is an interesting name: it seems to be a distortion (by a process known as 'folk etymology') of an earlier Aber Yau, 'the combined estuary', referring to the junction of the twin estuaries of the rivers, Glaslyn and Dwyryd. The place enters recorded history in the twelfth century, when Gerald of Monmouth wrote in 1188: 'We crossed the Traeth Mawr and the Traeth Bychan. These are two arms of the sea, one large and one small. Two stone castles have been built there recently. One called Castell Deudraeth belongs to the sons of Cynan and is situated in the Eifionydd area, facing the northern mountains.'

The sons of Cynan (Gruffydd and Maredudd) were princes who ruled large parts of north-west Wales. Their castle, which had various names over the centuries (including Castell Aber Yau and Castell Gwain Goch – after another local chieftain) is next mentioned by Edward Lloyd, writing in 1700, who reported that Aber Ia was then a small, isolated settlement with a foundry, a little shipyard, a handful of workers' cottages – and a castle.

Only one of these cottages (if there were more than one) has survived and it is incorporated in the plan of Portmeirion, as White Horses. The Mermaid, Salutation and the Mansion, which became the (later rebuilt)

Hotel, were constructed in the nineteenth century. The foundry, the shipyard and (if it was ever there) the water-mill are gone. Although the foundations may still be found in the woods to the west of Portmeirion, the castle was destroyed in 1869 or thereabouts by Sir William Fothergill Cook, inventor of the electric telegraph, 'lest its ruins should become known and attract visitors to the place'. Portmeirion attracts a good deal more than 200,000 visitors each year. *Thus, the whirligig of time brings in his revenges.*

Earlier in the century Aber Ia achieved a regrettable notoriety when one of the cottagers, Thomas Edwards – known as yr Hwntwr Mawr – was publicly hanged in Dolgellau in 1814 for the murder of Mary Jones, a maid at the nearby farm who had surprised him in the act of burglary. It is his cottage which has become White Horses today.

By 1850 the place seemed almost deserted. Writing in 1868, Richard Richards reports: 'Neither man nor woman was there, only a number of foreign water-fowl on a tiny pond, and two monkeys, which by their cries evidently regarded me as an unwelcome intruder. The garden itself was a very fine one, the walls of which were netted all over with fruit trees. Aber Ia, then, gentle reader, is a beautiful mansion on the shores of Traeth Bach in Merionethshire' – and, we may add, at least one (notorious) cottage on the water's edge, and the remains of a medieval castle.

The precise site of this demolished castle has been disputed. The old name of White Horses, the surviving cottage on the seashore beside The Observatory, was Tan-y-Castell, 'below the castle' – which seems to indicate a site on the hill immediately fronting the sea. An alternative site has been proposed further back on Battery Ridge at the point marked as 'the motte' on some old maps. The only surviving painting of the Castell perished in the fire at the architect's house in 1951. However, a recent archaeological survey has established that, beneath the walls erected to protect tourists by the architect, there are remains of the medieval castle on Battery Ridge. Moreover, a visiting water diviner has also found the source of the spring nearby which provided fresh water. The Castell Station is in the right place!

Readers may be confused by references to 'Castell Deudraeth': there are two, the demolished medieval castle on Battery Ridge mentioned by Gerald of Monmouth, and the modern Castell, located to the east of Portmeirion near the car-park, and built around 1840 by David Williams, solicitor and M P, who was the great-uncle of the architect of Portmeirion: his son, Sir Osmond Williams, M P, who inherited both the Castell and Aber Ia, in due time invited his nephew to survey the site. The rest is history.

When the architect bought the estate from his uncle in 1925 – for £4,000 – it was, in his words, 'a neglected wilderness – long abandoned by those romantics who had realised the unique appeal and possibilities of this

[11]

favoured promontory, but who had been carried away ... into sorrowful bankruptcy'. These hopeful speculators fall into two groups: the miners and the landscapers. There is evidence that Aber Ia harboured both a lead mine and a gold mine in the early nineteenth century. Neither prospered, though both yielded traces of metal – which might still be lying beneath the surface awaiting discovery.

But before turning to the first period of the construction of Portmeirion (1925–45), one should add a word about the estate, as it developed in the nineteenth century – and then declined after 1880. The owner, David Williams, who had built and dwelt in the modern Castell, seems to have given a free hand to a succession of tenants at Aber Ia, who proceeded to transform it.

The first was Henry Seymour Westmacott, who built the Mansion (now the Hotel) as a gentleman's residence, which he furnished lavishly in high Victorian style, together with the buildings which provided stables and a gardener's cottage for the estate – and which are now Portmeirion's Salutation and Mermaid. A keen horticulturalist, he was the designer of the garden that so impressed Richard Richards. Sadly he died in 1861 before he had time to enjoy what he had made.

His successor, Sir William Fothergill Cook, who demolished the medieval Castell to deter tourists, was also a horticulturalist: he laid out the paths and wild garden in the Gwyllt, and introduced many of the exotic species which can still be seen there – Monkey Puzzles. Cherry Laurels, varieties of rhododendrons and azaleas, as well as pines, hollies and other native trees and flowers. Many of these survive today in the Gwyllt, which became – and remains – a remarkable wild garden.

The third tenant was Mrs Adelaide Haig, mistress of Aber Ia from the 1880s until her death in 1917 and an extreme conservationist. She was truly eccentric, a naturist who lived in seclusion with her two sons and three daughters – and a staff of three. She preferred dogs to people. It is said that she kept her noisy mongrel pack in the elegant Mirror Room of the Mansion, and read them sermons from behind a screen.

She it was who created the Dogs' Cemetery, and decreed that no plant or tree or animal should be killed on her estate. In consequence, the Gwyllt became a real wilderness. When she died, the hearse that came to collect her remains was unable to reach the house until the driveway, completely overgrown, was cleared of trees and branches. After her death, a mysterious stag appeared at Aber Ia and threaded its way through the wilderness, rediscovering much of the twenty miles of pathways that had been laid out half a century earlier.

Her son, Caton Haig, a leading authority on Himalayan plants and trees, continued to be responsible for the development of the woodland. When he died in 1941, the Gwyllt was acquired by Clough Williams-Ellis who, together with his daughter, Susan, continued to maintain, manage and develop 'the wilderness' after the end of the Second World War. There was one final tenant of Aber Ia, between Mrs Haig and the advent of the architect of Portmeirion. His name is unknown; he apparently vanished shortly after signing the lease!

Aber Ia was a place where a succession of owners and tenants pursued their dreams. The sons of Cynan sought power; the miners and the shipwright (and the thief) wealth; the Victorians sought genteel seclusion in a managed, but natural, environment; Portmeirion is also a dream made real.

Since childhood, Clough Williams-Ellis had dreamed of becoming an architect and town planner. 'Some day, somewhere,' (he wrote) 'I would ... erect a whole group of buildings on my own chosen site for my own satisfaction.' At first, he had imagined that he would find an appropriate island site for what he called the Portmeirion Idea. He investigated more than twenty possible islands, but none seemed quite right. Although he lived only a few miles away (at Plas Brondanw, the family home for over four centuries), the seclusion and isolation of Aber Ia was so extreme that he knew it only from report and views across the estuary – until the day his uncle invited him to visit the place and advise him on how it might be let. The nephew saw at once that he had at last found the perfect site for the realisation of his dream.

He bought it in 1925, renamed it Portmeirion, and opened it to the public in 1926. The name, reminiscent of Portofino in Italy, which had in part inspired his work, is a combination of Port (because of the coastal location) and Meirion (the Welsh name of Merioneth, the old name of the county now known as Gwynedd). At that stage, the village consisted of no more than the Mansion, which he had adapted to provide an unlicensed hotel, the newly converted gardener's cottage (The Mermaid) and stables (Salutation), and two new cottages (Angel and Neptune). During the earlier construction period (1925–45) Portmeirion grew fast, with the addition of new buildings and the extension of the site both westwards and eastwards. Castell Deudraeth, together with its estate, was purchased in 1931 after the death of the architect's uncle; and the Gwyllt was acquired ten years later.

The rate of growth of Portmeirion at this time is astonishing; 1925 – Watch House; 1926 – The Hotel, The Mermaid, Salutation, Angel and Neptune; 1927 – Battery (and Chart Room); 1928 – Bell Tower, Government House; 1929 – Toll House, Prior's Lodging; 1930 – Pilot House, extension of the Hotel, Amis Réunis; 1931 – Salutation converted to provide a café; 1933–34 – Trinity, Dolphin; 1936 – Anchor, Observatory Tower; 1937 – Chantry, Fountain, The Town Hall; 1938–39 – Lady's Lodge. And then the War came.

The business model of Portmeirion is almost as interesting as its architecture. It earns its income, of course, from tourists – of two kinds: day-visitors and overnight residents. From the start it was essential that the Hotel and the increasing number of lodgings should not only pay their way, but also provide a surplus to

[13]

fund the next stage of construction. And, thanks to the energy of the creator of Portmeirion, they did so – and still do. However, it has often been something of a struggle to pay the bills. The initial purchase was funded by a loan from the Midland Bank, which perhaps deserves a plaque in recognition of that far-sighted investment! And, even today, visitors are told that Portmeirion remains something of a hand-to-mouth enterprise.

For many years, the number of visitors to Portmeirion each day was ingeniously controlled by price. A notice at the entrance informed them of the toll, as follows: 'In order sufficiently to discourage visitors to Portmeirion and to keep their numbers within acceptable limits, it has been found necessary to impose a toll of . Those wishing to avoid this impost are advised to turn back here.' The gap was a circular hole, behind which a red disc bearing a sequence of sums, could be adjusted. When King Edward VIII came while he was Prince of Wales, the figure shown was 10/- (ten shillings); apparently it kept the crowds away.

The architect was an effective publicist, and well-connected. The list of visitors is impressive: it includes Noel Coward (who wrote *Blithe Spirit* in The Fountain in a week), Bertrand Russell, Bernard Shaw and H. G. Wells; Rose Macaulay, Daphne du Maurier and John Steinbeck; A. P. Herbert, Osbert Lancaster and Gilbert Harding; Thor Heyerdahl, Peter Scott and Arthur Koestler; William Walton, Arthur Bliss and Gerald Moore; Lloyd George, Lord Boothby and Richard Crossman; several kings, queens and princes; and many other celebrities of all varieties. Among the architects who have visited and approved Portmeirion are Frank Lloyd Wright, Lord Esher and Lewis Mumford.

The new name took some time to establish itself – and find its place on official maps. Indeed, the first map to recognise Portmeirion was made in Germany shortly before the Second World War in preparation for their planned invasion of Britain. Fortunately, it was never required. But war brought a halt to the ambitious building programme. By this time the grand plan of Portmeirion was clearly defined, the whole site had been pegged out and many of the major landmarks were in place – the Hotel, Toll House, Town Hall and Bell Tower, for example.

Inevitably, the War and its aftermath brought a halt to the development of the village. Most of the construction team and staff of Portmeirion were called up for the duration. For a time, it was planned to requisition the village as a rest centre for RAF air crews on leave. But, because of distance, this idea was abandoned. Nonetheless, the architect kept the place open throughout the War as a sort of 'unofficial leave centre': many pilots (including the dam-buster, Guy Gibson) came to Portmeirion to enjoy its amenities and hospitality, which included dinghy-sailing in the estuary, flying model aeroplanes from the cliffs and naked bathing from the Beach – to the distress of the chapel-going local people.

Pictures from the National Gallery were stored at this time for safety in an old slate-mine near Portmeirion. The Director, Sir Kenneth Clark, was a regular visitor to the Hotel on his tours of inspection. At one stage during the War it was feared that the enemy might mount an invasion of Britain from Ireland and land its tanks in North Wales, perhaps even at Portmeirion itself. Blocks of granite were put in place on the roadway above the Hotel – and then quickly removed, when it became clear that they would prevent the delivery of beer to supply the soldiers stationed there. These blocks were later incorporated in Portmeirion's eclectic design to make a grand terrace wall near The Pantheon, where they remain to this day. Even in wartime, Portmeirion continued to function as a patron of the arts – and a source of good humour and fun.

It was some years before the development of the village could be restarted: planning restrictions were tight and finance difficult to find. But gradually life became easier and the second development phase (1945– 76) began. Once again, the rate of progress seems astonishing: 1954 – the Grotto; 1954–55 – Gate House; 1958 – Telford's Tower; 1959 – the Bristol Colonnade, Bridge House; 1959–60 the Round House; 1960 – Hercules Statue, the Belvedere; 1960–61 – The Pantheon; 1961 – the Bandstand; 1962–63 – Chantry Row, the Triumphal Arch; 1963 – the Lighthouse; 1963–64 – Arches; 1964 – Unicorn; 1964–65 – the Gloriette; 1965 – The Piazza, the Gothic Pavilion; 1966–67 – the Villa Winch; 1969 – Chantry Lodge, Cliff House; 1971 – the Seconds Warehouse; 1976 – the (southern) Toll Booth. This modest structure was the architect's last building: he died in 1978, aged almost 95.

As the renown of Portmeirion grew, the number of visitors increased and it became a popular venue for all kinds of people and all sorts of events; as has been said, Noel Coward, stayed here in 1941 and wrote *Blithe Spirit* in the space of five days; Guy Gibson, of 'dam-buster' fame, spent his last leave here during the Second World War. Scenes for *The Inn of the Sixth Happiness*, with Ingrid Bergman, were filmed in 1958; Patrick McGoohan's mysterious TV series, *The Prisoner*, was made here in 1966/67, vastly increasing Portmeirion's footfall; during the investiture of Prince Charles, in 1968, the government requisitioned Portmeirion to accommodate its official guests; over the years, various well-known people, such as Earl Russell and Sir Hugh Casson, have laid foundation stones and/or opened buildings and, as recently as 2001, the Welsh baritone, Bryn Terfel, opened the re-furbished Castell Deudraeth as a hotel.

In the years following the architect's death, relatively little has been added in the village, and almost nothing has been changed. The Toilets were built in 1979. The disastrous Hotel fire of 1981 necessitated a total reconstruction and restoration, which was aided by the architect's thorough description of the building in his own writings. It was reopened in 1988.

[15]

Clough's daughter, Susan, who created Portmeirion Pottery, had always been the leader in the development of the Gwyllt: she added the Gazebo in 1983, the Chinese Pagoda and Bridge in 1990, and the Classical Temple in 1992; her last contribution was Flora's Pergola in 2006. The (second, northern) Toll Booth had been added in 1999. What else? The proposed Lion Tower remains a dream. At the time of writing there is a plan to restore and reopen the Ferryman's Cottage at the extreme western tip of the Gwyllt to provide lodgings for visitors who seek almost total isolation (see p. 124). Until recently, it has been let to a musician who wished to practise her instrument unobserved and undisturbed.

It is inevitable – and appropriate – that after so many years of inspiration, innovation and creativity Portmeirion should pass through a period of conservation and relative inactivity. But, as cities like Oxford, Paris or Venice demonstrate, these quiescent periods also pass. We predict that future generations of guardians of the Portmeirion heritage will begin again to develop and redevelop the site and the village. What lives, must change; this law is true of all living things, plants, animals, people, communities, villages and cities – both the natural and the built environment. One day, it must also prove true for Portmeirion. (JE)

2. SIR CLOUGH WILLIAMS-ELLIS

Function or folly? Is there no third way,
fusing what's useful with what pleases? Here,
this sweet community of buildings, near
the sea and nestling in the hill's side, may
provide an answer! Spend a thoughtful day
amongst these painted walls designed to cheer
a grey Welsh sky – or sad grey lives. Revere
Clough Williams-Ellis, as you go away.

Cherish the past, he taught, *adorn the present*,
construct things *for the future* – which he did.
Si monumentum requiris, I bid
you look around. He found his lifelong duty
building this parable – for prince, or peasant.
Admire *that strange necessity*, called beauty.

CLOUGH WILLIAMS-ELLIS WAS A REMARKABLE CHARACTER WHO, during a long life (he died in 1978 a few weeks before his 95th birthday) accomplished much. If he were only remembered as Portmeirion's inspirational creator – he described it as a 'propagandist architectural adventure' – that would be sufficient. But he achieved so much more, claiming to have had an 'unfairly generous allowance of good luck'. He was a lecturer, speechmaker, broadcaster, author of many articles and books, predominantly on architecture and town and country planning, but also wrote the history of the Tank Corps and two autobiographies. He was a tireless campaigner for the protection of rural Britain and the establishment of National Parks, a great supporter of the National Trust and a fashionable architect, with numerous buildings and their surrounding landscapes to his credit. He travelled widely, was an adventurous sailor, a country landowner and a serving officer during the First World War with a distinguished war record. His was a busy, well spent life.

I have read and much enjoyed both his autobiographies, *Architect Errant,* published in 1971, and *Around the World in Ninety Years,* published in 1978 shortly after he had died. Both books are unrelentingly cheerful and delightfully self-deprecating. He never claimed to have made his own luck but I have concluded that this, together with his boundless optimism, is the key to understanding his many successes. He was self-assured (he, of course, claimed it was arrogance), doggedly persistent in pursuing his vision, never afraid to ask, adept at spotting and seizing opportunities and a courageous risk taker. His formal architectural training amounted to a mere three months (apparently Edwin Lutyens' reaction was, 'What, you took three months! Why, I was through with it all in three weeks!'). Largely self-taught, he claimed to depend on 'an intuitive and instinctive feeling for proportion, propriety, scale, setting, use and apt materials'.

Clough Williams-Ellis, born in 1883, was the fourth of six sons. His father was a scholar and country parson much given to reading Greek and Latin texts and to solving mathematical and chess problems. The family moved from Gayton in Northamptonshire to North Wales when Clough was four years old. He used to accompany his mother on leisurely, meandering walks during which she would enthuse about ordinary things such as the green moss on boulders and the golden lichen on some worn steps of an old stile. Observing these small details, together with his mother showing him how to sketch Welsh cottages, seduced the young Clough and by the age of six he had set his heart on becoming an architect.

Initially Clough and his brothers were educated by a governess. Not very successfully, it seems. Clough remembers 'those interminable, leaden hours of half-learning and blank not-learning'. When he was thirteen, Clough was packed off to Oundle where he excelled at science and geometry but not at anything else. He says he finished his schooldays as a 'bigoted Philistine'. After his father had provided some extra tuition (he says he can't remember feeling grateful) he went to Cambridge, allegedly chosen in preference to Oxford because the gowns were blue rather than black. He started to read for the natural sciences tripos but left voluntarily after a year of 'not much work but plenty of social contacts and enjoyment'.

For a short while he was apprenticed, at the suggestion of a second-cousin, to a country builder where 'I learnt as fast as I could be shown how'. Determined to become an architect, he looked up 'architecture' in the London telephone directory and discovered the Architectural Institute. The next day he walked into the Institute unannounced and asked to see the principal who, impressed with the young man's obvious enthusiasm, accepted him to study to become a qualified architect.

Having completed just two terms at the Institute, a relative offered Clough his first architectural commission; to build a country home for a charitable institution near Oxford. Working on the project was so time-consuming that he was formally asked to devote himself to his studies or leave the Institute. He chose to leave: 'I cheerfully cut myself adrift from the training ship'. Despite having no qualifications, only his unwavering passion, he set himself up as an architect with an office in London.

His father gave him a small allowance of £160 a year and, using his contacts, small commissions came his way. When times were quiet, he plugged the gaps by inventing and patenting things such as an electric starting switch, an automatic air-lock serving-hatch and a novel chair that was successfully marketed by Heals.

As I have read about Clough's eventful life I have noticed how often he describes significant events as 'out of the blue' coincidences. He modestly claims that they were all sheer luck but I suspect the coincidences happened too often to be dismissed so lightly. My theory is that Clough was brilliant at making and taking opportunities; an opportunist in the best sense of the word. Consider the following examples.

He met his future wife 'coincidentally' at a meeting of the Housing Association and, in order to have an excuse to see more of her, accepted a challenge, extended by his future father-in-law, to design and build a cottage at the lowest price. He won the competition (by building a four-roomed cottage for only £101) and a wife, Amabel Strachey, who went on to become a well-known author of children's fairy stories and other publications, some co-authored with her husband.

As a subaltern during the First World War, Clough, with his propensity for sketching landscapes, got himself 'borrowed' by Divisional HQ and became an Intelligence Officer producing drawings of the enemy's defences, often from an observation balloon. He had to work fast, only being allowed up for thirty minutes, because it generally took the Germans about that time to decide the balloon was worth shooting down and to train their guns on the target. Clough, of course, asserts that coming through the War unscathed was 'pure luck'.

SIR CLOUGH WILLIAMS-ELLIS

A commission to convert Stowe for use as a school came, he claims, 'out of the blue'. But in fact, the invitation directly resulted from an impressive article about Stowe that he had written for *The Spectator*. Converting the vast building into a functioning school was a huge undertaking and the chief benefactor became difficult and unreliable. Clough, however, had the staunch support of the headmaster, J. F. Roxburgh, whom he had 'bullied into putting in for the job'. The governors, strapped for cash, decided to sell off various artefacts and not to buy the approach to the school, the mile and a half long Grand Avenue. So, Clough, convinced it must be saved from ribbon development, bought it himself.

It is remarkable how often Clough met, entirely 'by coincidence', influential people during train journeys. This is the way he landed his first big job in 1912. He describes it thus: 'It all began, as did finding my wife, with an encounter that was so much of a coincidence that few novelists would dare to use it'. The man he met on the train was travelling to London to find an architect to build him a new house on the site of his dilapidated castle. Clough became responsible for the building of a fine country house with gardens, stables, garages, power-house and cottages on the banks of the River Wye in Breconshire. Furthermore, the client was not only wealthy but appreciative: 'I was not hurried and there was no deadline'. A dream commission, from which Clough never really looked back.

A well-known example of Clough's luck and opportunism was, of course, the purchase, in 1925, of the estate that became the site for his Portmeirion venture. 'One day, entirely unexpectedly, an absentee uncle, Sir Osmond Williams of Deudraeth Castle, asked me if I knew of anyone who would care to buy an adjoining secondary coastal property of his which, though only five miles from my own home, I had never seen except from the sea ... It had all that I had ever dreamed of as desirable for my perfect site – beetling cliffs and craggy pinnacles, level plateaux and little valleys, a tumbling cascade, splendid old trees and exotic flowering shrubs; a coastline of rocky headlands, caves and sandy bays.'

As you explore Portmeirion, Clough's experiment in 'architectural good manners', you might like to apply the five criteria described in his and Amabel's book *The Pleasures of Architecture,* published in 1924. Ask, not necessarily of each building, but rather of the collection as a whole:

1. Do you fulfil your function adequately and with the minimum of friction?
2. Are you structurally efficient?
3. Do you seem beautiful to me?
4. Have you got a general architectural theme which you try to express?
5. Are you a good neighbour?

They add, 'Candidates for admiration need not necessarily pass in all five questions.'

[21]

In 1958 Clough was awarded a CBE for 'public services' and, in 1972, was knighted for 'services to the preservation of the environment and to architecture'. At the time he was the oldest person ever to be knighted. In his final book, written when he was 94, he acknowledges his persistent good luck and his single-mindedness. 'I have never seriously wavered from my passionately loved profession of architecture, landscape and design.' Indeed, at the age of 90, having announced his retirement, he received his last commission from a young couple who had inherited an extensive estate in Cumbria, Dalton Hall. This involved the demolition of the old house which had active dry-rot, and the building of a spacious house and gardens. Sir Clough describes it as a 'satisfying last fling'.

Sir Clough, a larger than life character, was cheerful to the end. He did not, however, relish going to Heaven because 'it is supposed to be perfect, and so leaves no scope for me to improve its appearance!' (PH)

3. THE WALKS

       Some fifty yards ahead
they find the way through mist – without a map:
as far behind, she points out paths to left
and right they might, or should, have taken. I
carry the compass, read the map, between
my wife and friends – and wonder if I am
         the leader or the led?

       I see that, as we stride
or stumble through our lives, our family
and friends – alongside, following, in front –
encourage us, advise, suggest, deplore
the paths we choose, while we – lost in the mist –
stand puzzled and alone – and in our hands
         no compass, map or guide.

WE HAVE PLANNED THE LAYOUT OF THIS BOOK TO PROVIDE A SEQUENCE OF SEVEN WALKS THROUGH – and around – Portmeirion. Each begins where the previous one ends, so that they form a single (if severely distorted) circular walk. They take the reader past, or close to, each of the 45 buildings and locations identified as of special interest in the excellent official guide-book (Robin Llywelyn's *Portmeirion*). Most have stimulated the paintings and poems printed here: but the rest are also worth a good deal more than a passing glance. We have added the guide-book number of the sights, as they occur in our book.

The first walk starts at the Tollgate [1], twin booths on either side of the road as you approach the village from the car park. It follows the main street down the hill in a long reversed S-bend until it reaches the Hotel [43] and the sea at the bottom. The second takes the reader back up the hill by a slightly different – and more direct – route across the Piazza [26]. As it approaches the top of the hill again, we invite the reader to follow the third walk (take care!) down a steep, stony path (with wonderful views of the estuary) to reach the sea once more and follow the path along the water's edge to the Stone Boat [42].

The fourth follows Portmeirion's designated Coastal Walk from the Stone Boat [42] to the Lighthouse on the point and then turns uphill through the woods to double back towards Portmeirion. It brings you back to the village past the Playhouse (or AV Room [38]), where you may view a presentation by the architect about the history, design and construction of Portmeirion. The fifth follows Portmeirion's designated Forest Walk back into the woods in a loop along higher ground, which brings you back once more to a point where you may re-enter the village, if you choose.

Or you might turn back into the woods and explore the Gwyllt, the deeper and less accessible woodland to the west. This is the longest of the seven walks, but it is also designed to bring the reader back along a section of the Forest Walk to re-enter Portmeirion at the Playhouse [38]. The seventh – and final walk – begins close by at the Triumphal Arch [34] and follows the main street up the hill past the entrance to the car park. (JE)

4. THE CHOICE OF THE SIGHTS

The more we judge, the less we understand:
the less we find we choose not to misjudge;
the more we're likely to misunderstand.
The less we understand, the more we judge.

Choice is a discipline we ought to learn.
(An ice-cream? Chocolate or vanilla – choose!)
Poor choice: a habit so hard to unlearn.
Our work, our mate, our home, our lives – we choose.

The more we understand, the less we judge:
the less we're likely to misunderstand;
the more we find we choose not to misjudge.
The less we judge, the more we understand.

ONE IS SPOILT FOR CHOICE AT PORTMEIRION: there is so much to see, to admire and wonder about. We have, of course, chosen our favourite buildings and views, arranging them to punctuate the seven walks this book is designed around. We apologise if we have omitted a sight you particularly love, Watch House or the Woodland Train, for example. Because of the constraints of space and our desire not to make the book too heavy to carry around the village, we have sadly had to abandon some of the poems and paintings we had hoped to include. Perhaps, one day, we shall find an opportunity to use them elsewhere.

We have sought to choose sights that would enable us to make a pleasing picture and an interesting poem. Sometimes the artist chose the sight; sometimes the poet. Part of the challenge and enjoyment of creating this book has been the demands we have made upon each other. 'Make a picture of a flagpole – and the elusive Ghost Garden!' 'Write a poem about the AV Room – and the Toilets!' In practice, the poem usually (but not always) came first, so the poet must bear the greater responsibility for any apparent mistakes of selection.

The poem suggests that poor choice is a bad habit some of us fall into, a kind of behavioural disorder. The sad news is that our choices determine our lives, so the habit of making poor choices will prove a heavy burden. The good news is that we can always learn how to choose wisely. It is never too late. For our part, we hope our readers will feel that our choices, if not perfect, are at least good enough to provide a pleasing introduction to this very special place. (JE)

[27]

5. THE POEMS

Greek yoghurt, cream with attitude, requires
a contrast, marmalade or strawberries –
something with colour, something sweet and sunny,
or tart, with texture. Sensual discord fires
the synapses. My favourite topping is
        a teaspoonful of honey.

Of all the insects only bees provide
food humans eat. A dozen bees will take
six weeks (their lifespan) for a ceremony
of harvest, dance, disposal, multiplied
a thousand times – twelve maiden-slaves – to make
        one teaspoonful of honey.

Poets are apian, storing bric-a-brac,
bee-alchemists, who turn dust into gold.
We do not value our achievements, money
or honours half as much as this strange knack,
sweet skill, of transformation. Here – behold –
        my teaspoonful of honey.

I DON'T THINK POETS HAVE MADE A VERY GOOD JOB OF EXPLAINING WHAT POETRY IS. They either say something rather trite, or something almost incomprehensible. Coleridge called it 'the best words in the best order'; Shelley said it was 'the record of the best and happiest moments of the happiest and best minds'; Wordsworth memorably described it as 'the spontaneous overflow of powerful feelings – it takes its origin from emotion recollected in tranquillity'; while Carl Sandburg tells us that 'poetry is the achievement of the synthesis of hyacinths and biscuits'; and Wendy Cope observes that 'sometimes poetry is emotion recollected in a highly emotional state'. Hmm.

My aim, when writing verse, is to say something worth remembering – in a way that makes it memorable. In other words, I try to express something striking in an arresting way. (I hope the reader may be able to recognise this.) I agree with Robert Frost, who apparently once remarked that he'd 'as soon write free verse as play tennis with the net down'. These poems are therefore written in what is called formal verse: they have measured lines, stanzaic structure, rhyme or alliteration to give them shape and make them easier to remember. Some are written in blank (unrhymed) verse, or in a stress-measured alliterative line that was the rule in Old English. Several of the poems in this collection are sonnets, or double sonnets; there is also one sestina. I like intricate forms. I hope, before I die, to write a few poems that some readers will think worth learning by heart. (JE)

6. THE PAINTINGS

Paul Gauguin used to call himself a Sunday painter –
  until the day he ditched the day-job (banking),
  abandoned wife and children, started painting
  not what he saw, but what he felt; met Vincent
  Van Gogh (who died), and sailed away to settle
  down in Tahiti, where he painted naked
  young native women – badly. Gauguin's careful
early Parisian (weekend) work strikes me as better!

I like those eager Sunday painters with their precious
  pictures in public parks hanging on railings.
  Warm summer weekends bring them out in dozens –
  like ladybirds, or dandelions, or litter,
  enlivening the landscape's greens and browns and
  greys – as they sit and watch the curious passers-
  by, hoping someone some day sees what they saw,
feels what they felt, and purchases one of their pictures.

For fifty years I was a sort of Sunday poet –
  my verse produced like an occasional table
  to celebrate a rare and special moment,
  until I followed Gauguin's lead, devoted
  myself full-time to search for words and phrases
  to represent my visions and my feelings.
  Language and images transform the occurring
world: that is why the world needs poetry and painting.

I LOVE PAINTING WATERCOLOURS, both for the struggle to get the paints to behave and for the eventual outcome. I describe it as a struggle because, unlike oils and acrylics where you can add layers and make alterations almost indefinitely, watercolours are less forgiving. Getting watercolours to do what I want them to do is what really intrigues me. Too much fiddling makes them muddy and dull. As the painting develops, I frequently prop it up and stand back to take a long hard look. Sometimes I leave the room and return suddenly to catch the painting unawares when, just for a split second, I see it with a fresh pair of eyes.

Usually a painting will pass through a stage where I'm convinced I will have to abandon it and start again. Knowing when to quit and when to persevere is, for me, part of the fascination with the whole process and, as in life, perseverance usually pays off. When I'm painting I enjoy a feeling of 'flow' where I am so engrossed that nothing can intrude (except meal times – a corner of the table is often my studio!). Mostly I paint buildings and landscapes which is why Portmeirion and the peninsular was such an instant attraction; I share Sir Clough's love of buildings and trees. Sometimes I paint outside balancing on my little canvas stool, but, sadly, my visits to Portmeirion have not been long enough and I have therefore had to rely on quick sketches and copious photographs to use as references.

Producing the paintings of Portmeirion has been fun. It has made me look harder than I otherwise might have done, to delight in so many of the small details and to giggle at Sir Clough's little jokes; the absurdly theatrical Bus Stop (see p. 100) built of corrugated iron being one of many examples. I have enjoyed the cheerful colours of the buildings (never before using so much turquoise!) and the magnificent views in the forest and the Gwyllt.

I hope you like my paintings and feel they do justice to the spirit of Portmeirion. I wonder if Sir Clough would approve? (PH)

[31]

7. AFTERWORD

Some things you have you cannot hold –
  sunshine, delight or youth.
All golden things are mere fool's gold:
  this is an ancient truth.

Those treasured rings, rich yellow cloth,
  must soon reveal their rust,
the damage from the hungry moth
  which crumbles all to dust.

There is no other life to come.
  Time's arrow won't allow
us golden moments, once we're dumb.
  Heaven is here, and now.

WE FIRST SAW PORTMEIRION TWO YEARS AGO IN 2013, when on holiday together in Anglesey. Our wives wanted to visit the village: we wanted to climb Snowdon. They won. Once we arrived here and saw the remarkable achievement of the architect and builders of Portmeirion, we fell in love (as we hope our readers have, or will) with Portmeirion's strange beauty. And so we have dedicated this book to Carol and Wendy, with our thanks. Since that year we have visited Portmeirion several times to help us prepare this text, compose these verses, and paint these pictures. We hope that time will grant us many more visits in the years ahead. And we also hope our book may encourage others to make the trip to North Wales to marvel at the sights of Portmeirion in its sublime setting.

This is the third volume in what I hope will become a series of such books about places worthy of note. The first two, which presented the sights of Oxford and of London, were illustrated by Katharine Shock: *That Sweet City* (2013) and *That Mighty Heart* (2014). I hope to persuade other artists, and other poets, to contribute to the series. The next volume will be devoted to the spa town of Buxton.

Peter and I are deeply grateful to the Trustees of Portmeirion, and in particular to Robin Llywelyn, for permission (and encouragement) to write this book as a small act of homage to a great man and his fine achievement, one of the wonders of Wales. We never met Clough Williams-Ellis: we wish we had. In these paintings and poems we have tried to echo the spirit of his creative and playful imagination.

We are also most grateful to James Ferguson, our brave and generous publisher, who believes that readers will wish to buy this book, as they have its two predecessors. We hope he proves to be right. We also want to thank the designer, Andrew Esson, for helping us get this far. Several members of our respective families and friends have offered us helpful comments, valuable corrections and kind encouragement: we thank them all.

But, above all, we hope that you, our gentle readers, will enjoy the book, visit the sights of Portmeirion, explore the walks and study our poems and paintings. Meanwhile, we can report that during our most recent visit we have also found time to climb Snowdon! (JE)

[33]

W N S E

Portmeirion

(40)

The Angel (31)

Hotel (43)

The Piazza (26)

Telford's Tower

(25) (36)

Bristol Colonnade (24)

Estuary

Bridge House (10)

(8)

(2)

Tollgate (1)

(3)

100 m

Walk 1 Tollgate to Hotel

I. THE TOLLGATE TO THE HOTEL

THE FIRST WALK STARTS AT THE TOLLGATE [1], close to the Coach and Car Parks. Pass between the twin booths, built on either side of the road, and proceed southwards past the Toilets [3] on the left-hand side, and the Pottery Shop (the Seconds Warehouse [2]) on the right, until the road starts to bend to the right. The route takes you beneath two houses built across the road Gate House [8] and BRIDGE HOUSE [10]. As you emerge, you find a splendid panorama of Portmeirion spread out before you. Follow the road round the corner, and then turn left down some steps into THE PIAZZA [26], which you should explore. Don't miss THE BRISTOL COLONNADE [24] beside the steps you descended. When ready, return to the road the way you came into The Piazza, turn left, and continue behind The Colonnade and round the corner until you reach TELFORD'S TOWER [36] on the right (opposite The Gloriette [25]. Now, follow the road round the sharp left-hand bend to find THE ANGEL [31] on your left opposite The Town Hall [40] (which features in Walk 2) and then continue down the hill towards the sea to reach THE HOTEL [43].

THE TOLLGATE

This pair of booths provides Portmeirion's
Tollgate: here's where you start your visit, pay
your dues, and find the first (and last) design –
the first you see, the last he built – the man
who made this place, Clough Williams-Ellis, who
loved pink and turquoise paint, Palladian
designs, and fun. Portmeirion's no joke,
but feel its smiling welcome as you step
into the village to explore its charms.
I promise you'll be smiling too when you
complete the tour, return here, and pass through
the Tollgate, pleased, surprised, impressed, replete.

BRIDGE HOUSE

Bridge House, known locally as *Carlton House*
Terrace, has 'classical formality'
(the architect explained) to contrast with
the picturesque Toll House which stands nearby.
(Look at the urns which decorate the roof.)

I like most architecture, but I love
classical buildings like this. Symmetry
is satisfying: the façade, designed
to face the setting sun, delights the eye.
I smile to see a house above a road!

Portmeirion's a treasure-house of art
and artifice and architecture, which
you'll never tire of. Bees to blossom, those
who make art, poets, painters, and the rest,
and those who practise crafts, we all come here.

[39]

The Piazza

I love this little square – the flowers, the pool,
the fountain, and those turquoise benches where
the visitor may rest, reflect and share
an ice-cream or an insight, although you'll
not find it quite like this – without some people there.

Piazzas demand people, as a stage
requires some players and an audience
to animate the place. The sounds and scents
of human life are needed to engage
the artist's eye and hand, the poet's eloquence.

Where have they gone? Just look around. A child
was splashing in the pool a moment past,
an old man dozed, two women took a last
look round the square, a dozen mobiles filed
a million photos, as the August evening passed.

And now, the day is ended. Night consumes
the colours and the clarity of things.
The flowers and buildings fade. The darkness brings
a kind of death. An all-pervading gloom's
supreme. Another day departs on time's swift wings.

Where are the olden days, the times gone by?
All life must fade: not griefs, nor loves, endure.
We die. But paint and poetry mature.
Art lives. We shall not altogether die.
At least, a future for this precious book seems sure.

P 4

THE BRISTOL COLONNADE

Designed to form a noble frontispiece
to decorate a Bristol bathhouse three
long centuries ago, the stones you see,
bomb-damaged and defaced by time, once peace
returned to Europe, were transported – piece
by piece – to Wales, and here rebuilt to be
seen and admired once more by you and me.
And here, I hope, they long may rest in peace.

This Colonnade, with its entablature,
was reconstructed by a mason who
was master of his craft, a patient man
called William Davis. May his name endure,
together with his work, who read the plan,
then made it perfect for the world to view.

TELFORD'S TOWER

This Tower is dedicated to an engineer
(and architect) in celebration of his work,
on the occasion of his bi-centenary
in 1958 (a little late). Apart
from gods and demi-gods (like Neptune, Hercules,
and Trinity), mythical creatures (Unicorn,
Angel and Mermaid) or existing animals
(Dolphin and Horses), only Prior's Lodging takes
its name from someone real – apart from Telford's Tower.

Beside it there remains a space intended for
another tower, The Lion Tower, as yet unbuilt.
A lion of an architect has honoured here
this lion of an engineer who built canals
and churches, roads and docks – and bridges (more
than thirty); *and* he also wrote some decent verse!
Two towers – two lions – two great craftsmen, here conjoined,
Clough Williams-Ellis, Thomas Telford: what a pair!
(I wonder if one day we'll see that Lion Tower?)

[46]

THE ANGEL

I watch the angel watching over me,
carved in pale stone, patient in frozen flight,
across the street. From where I wait I see
the figure shine in sunlight, glow by night.

Michael or Gabriel or Raphael – who
is the true guardian-angel of my life?
In turn, a soldier, teacher, artist too –
at least in words – I ask my angel-wife.

'There are no roads,' she says, 'All roads are made
by walking.* So, there are no angels; angels
are humans in disguise – those not afraid
to challenge failure, transform wrongs and change ills.'

*An old Spanish proverb, reminding us that it's *people* who
make a difference.

THE HOTEL

Why, I wonder, is this hotel nameless?
  All those pretty houses have a name.
For a designation – is its claim less?
  Anonymity just seems a shame.

Massive Castell Deudraeth is distinguished
  by a label – *not* by its design!
If a hotel had to be extinguished,
  guess which choice of victim would be mine.

Though destroyed once in a conflagration,
  this hotel predates Portmeirion:
Aber Ia was in occupation
  long before the village was begun.

Mansions like it date from 1850.
  This old summer residence was well
on its way to ruin when the thrifty
  architect created this hotel.

Comfy beds, good food (we both have stayed here);
  gracious welcome from attentive staff;
prices? – fair enough, I wouldn't say *dear*.
  (Some would – like my careful better half!)

I just wish the hotel had a title.
  Not one building should be nameless here.
While it waits a new one, this prime site'll
  have to use the old name: Aber Ia.

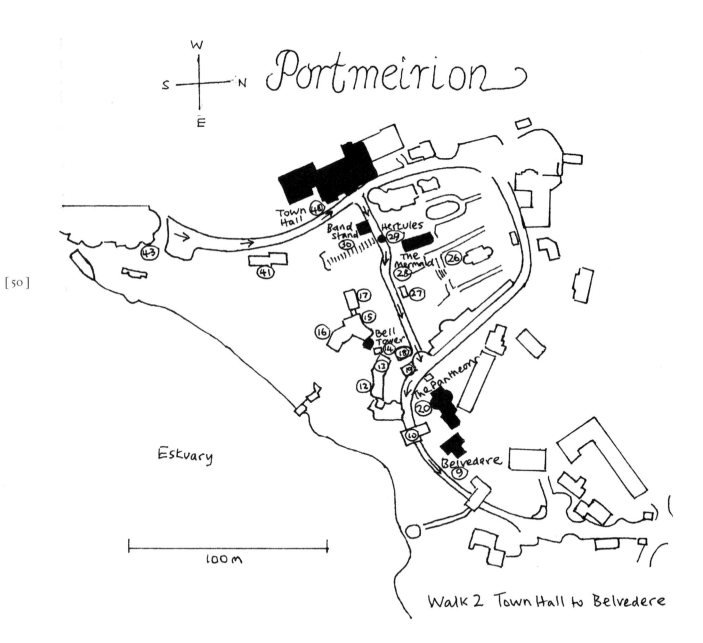

Portmeirion

Town Hall (40)
Band Stand (30)
Hercules (29)
The Mermaid (28)
(26)
(27)
(41)
(43)
(17)
(15)
(16)
Bell Tower (14)
(18)
(13)
(19)
(12)
The Pantheon
(20)
(10)
Belvedere (9)

Estuary

100 m

Walk 2 Town Hall to Belvedere

2. THE TOWN HALL TO THE BELVEDERE

THE SECOND WALK STARTS FROM THE HOTEL [43], which marked the end of Walk 1, and takes you back up the hill away from the sea. Passing The Anchor and Fountain [41] on the right, you should visit THE TOWN HALL [40] on the left, and then cross the roadway to enter The Piazza [26] and find THE BANDSTAND [30] on the right – and the HERCULES STATUE [29] – before you pass THE MERMAID [28] on the left. As you walk on, you pass The Gothic Pavilion [27] on the left and – to the right, and set back – The Dolphin [17], Government House [15] and – behind it – Watch House [16]. Don't miss the Stone Lion, erected to mark the architect's 90th birthday in 1973. Also on the right, set back from your path, is THE BELL TOWER [14]. Continue along the path (in an easterly direction) and go up the steps – noting The Round House [18] on the right – to reach the road. THE PANTHEON [20] is on the opposite side. Turn right up the hill, taking care not to miss Lady's Lodge [19], Prior's Lodging [13] and Battery [12] on the right hand side; then pass beneath Bridge House [10] to find THE BELVEDERE [9] on your left.

The Town Hall

'The most substantial' and, perhaps, 'the most
successful building at Portmeirion',
the guide-book claims. This is no idle boast:
find me a greater or a finer one!
[52]   This Hall provides a venue for a do –
a wedding or a concert or a dance.
Admire the grand room – and its ceiling. You
may wonder how, and by what chance,
it was transported here from Emral Hall
to save it from destruction. (Read the book!)*
Or, better still, stand here and study all
its beauties – floor and wall and window – look!
       'A home for fallen buildings'? No! This place
       is where they win redemption and new grace.

The family was not without disgrace,
   whose lovely ballroom Clough chose to displace
from Flintshire to Portmeirion. The book
reports the first and final owners' fall
from grace (one lynched, one mad) –
   but you should look
beyond such tempting tales to what I call
a modern miracle – the elegance
within, the gracefulness without, the view
this 'village hall' provides for those whose glance
is more than superficial – me or you!
The architect felt pleased with what was done –
because the Town Hall surely *is* the most
successful building at Portmeirion –
or anywhere along this lovely coast.

* Robin Llywelyn's *Portmeirion*, p.36.

THE BANDSTAND

Music's like electricity – it moves,
empowers, enlightens us. These truths allow a
conceit that this concealed sub-station proves
the power of music – and the strains of power ...

Gaze at this bandstand. Close your eyes – to hear
the sound of horns and trumpets, melody
and counterpoint, a silver band, the clear,
sweet, clement music of 'Deep Harmony'.

Deep peace enfolds the unborn child – then life
disrupts this harmony of nothingness.
Existence means disorder, pain and strife.
Presence and consciousness engender stress.

All daily life is disharmonious: light
brings conflict, duty, promises to keep.
Each day we welcome the return of night –
the deep, but transient, harmony of sleep.

After life's discord, order is restored.
For, as we draw that final, mortal breath,
We know that all shall earn a fair reward:
the deep, enduring harmony of death.

The music ends; the echoes die. And now,
open your eyes again to gaze and see
the architecture's frozen music – how
it forms Portmeirion's deep harmony.

[55]

HERCULES STATUE

'Quis hic locus, quae regio, quae mundi plaga?'

Look! Here's a hero, Hercules – half god,
half man: he's holding up the world on those
strong shoulders. *Why?* Because he had to steal
the apples of the three Hesperides,
the daughters of the evening – so he asked
for Atlas's assistance, and took on
the task of holding up the universe,
while Atlas pinched the apples for him. *Why?*
Those famous dozen labours were imposed
on Hercules by King Eurystheus: catch
a lion, kill the Hydra, hunt a stag –
and then a boar – spring-clean the stables, shoot
some birds, capture a bull – and then some mares –
go get the girdle of Hyppolita,
the Amazonian queen, and steal some cows –
and then those apples. Lastly, Hercules
was sent to fetch a dog (called Cerberus)
from hell. *But, why …?* Because he'd killed his wife
and children in a fit of madness … *Why,*
I want to know, is this strange statue here?
I see. Portmeirion's architect found him
in Aberdeen and brought him here to guard
the village square; the sculptor's William Brodie;
the sculpture now commemorates the best
of all Portmeirion's fine summers. *Why …?*

The Mermaid

Four buildings here predate Portmeirion –
And this is one. A mermaid's a queer fish:
this Mermaid, now providing rather swish
self-catering accommodation one
would love to share, was once a run—
down cottage for a gardener. I wish
I'd seen the monkeys with the standoffish
demeanour, who lived here, in rain or sun,
before Portmeirion was dreamed of. This
is what I love about this place – the fun,
the fanciful imagination and
the loving care with which it has been planned
and built. This is what makes Portmeirion
as rare and lovely as a mermaid's kiss.

[59]

THE BELL TOWER

Fewer towers than San Gimignano,
fewer bells than heaven, or Aberdovey,
still, Portmeirion – this Paradise – links
Wales and Italy. The Campanile,
planned, designed and built near the beginning
of the project – with its chiming clock, now
silent – is the focal point of the whole
enterprise. The architect provided
this 'dramatic gesture' to foreshadow
all the wonders that would follow in the
future – and they have. Just look around you!
Read the plaque placed near the base – and smile: the
castle of a king of Wales (and distant
ancestor of Clough's), which stood nearby once,
was demolished to prevent the ruins
from attracting tourists. Time revenges
wrongs; posterity redeems the past; and
those who study history learn wisdom.
(Clough's Portmeirion's designed for tourists!)

THE PANTHEON

Conscious, he said of 'dome deficiency',
the architect determined to provide
this great eight-sided Pantheon, and hide
its frontage with a porch – a gallery
for minstrels once in Cheshire. You may see
old prints with this strange structure taking pride
of place in some salon, where it supplied
heat – it's a fireplace! – and sweet harmony.

Nothing is here which fails to interest
the visitor – the makers and the things
they made, buildings, or pottery, their dreams
and this reality, those farfetched schemes
and this odd, reconstructed chimney breast,
the Pantheon's porch – where now no minstrel sings.

(Boredom's the worst of sins – or so I feel.
In action or in suffering, we must
eschew dullness: those bored, and bores, disgust.)
Family businesses like this reveal
what greater corporations can conceal:
familiar virtues, love and hope and trust –
and something more exciting, more robust,
a taste which make a feast from every meal.

Admire the father's dome, the daughter's cup.
Design delights, where beauty marries use.
(This place might make a poet pen a lecture!)
Like shredded lettuce, modern architecture
needs salad-dressing: add the lemon-juice
of inspiration – or just 'Clough it up'!

THE BELVEDERE

The Belvedere: self-catering; sleeps six; the house
is Classical; it has two storeys; and a view.
Notice the concrete balustrade in front!
At first 'The Fountain House', the name was changed because
The Fountain (by The Anchor) was already built.
Portmeirion's far-fetched and fanciful house-names
delight me: Angel, Arches, Battery, the three
called Chantry (Lodge and Row), Dolphin, Gazebo and
The Gothic Pavilion, Gate House, The Gloriette.
Consider Lady's Lodge, The Mermaid, Neptune; or
The Prior's House, The Pantheon, and Pilot House;
The Round House, Salutation, Toll House, Telford's Tower
and Trinity. Remember Unicorn, Watch House,
White Horses, Villa Winch. I doubt I've got them all!
Where's Hercules, The Bristol Colonnade, Bridge House,
The Bell Tower or Stone Boat? I see it isn't just
Portmeirion's strange architecture pleases me –
I have also fallen in love with these buildings' names.

[65]

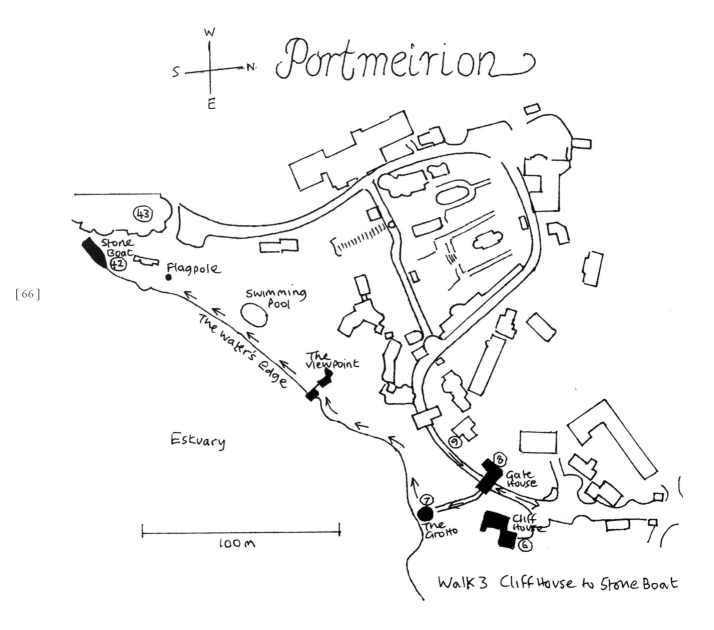

Portmeirion

W
S — N
E

43

Stone
Boat
42

Flagpole

Swimming
Pool

The Water's Edge

The
Viewpoint

Estuary

100m

9

8
Gate
House

7
The
Grotto

Cliff
House
6

Walk 3 Cliff House to Stone Boat

3. CLIFF HOUSE TO THE STONE BOAT

THE THIRD WALK BEGINS AT CLIFF HOUSE [6], set back from the road on the right. Walk up to it from The Belvedere [9], the end of Walk 2. Now, walk back downhill to GATE HOUSE [8]; and then find the path (on the left) that leads to THE GROTTO [7]. Enjoy the view. Emerging from The Grotto, you will find a path which leads steeply downhill along the coastline back towards the Hotel [43]. Follow this with care. Near the bottom, you will reach THE VIEWPOINT, before finally reaching level ground and THE WATER'S EDGE. Continue past the little swimming pool (on the right), with the sea on your left, until you pass THE FLAGPOLE on the right-hand side and finally reach the amazing STONE BOAT [42].

CLIFF HOUSE

[69]

Trompe l'oeil (like irony) creates a form
of artistic deception you can see
through, like the northern windows of Cliff House –
which can't be seen through, since they're painted on.
The style is Classical, with symmetry
of fenestration, but the privacy
of guests is still preserved by this device.

Trompe l'oeil provides some interest: blank walls
would seem a disappointment to the eye –
which much prefers to be deceived, than bored.
And yet, the viewer usually can tell
these windows are all fakes – and poets know
that irony is easily seen through.
For that's the point; to seem, but not to, fool.

GATE HOUSE

Built on bare rock, this Gate House is baroque
in character. The floodlit arch contains
a ceiling-mural by Hans Feibusch and
(up high) those sham green shutters are just painted on.

[70]

Entrance and exit, Gate House sees a flock
of visitors, who shelter from the rain's
assault on Welsh days. Since it was first planned,
and built, it's harboured thousands who have come and gone.

Portmeirion's a place that's built on rock,
as houses should be. Matthew's text explains
what happens to a house that's built on sand.
Don't miss the lessons hidden here you come upon.

THE GROTTO

I love this little house of shells: the view
commands the estuary. The astrolabe
invites discussion. *What's it for?* – To help
locate the sun and stars in ancient times.
(Chaucer once wrote a treatise on the thing.)
I think it's only ornamental here.

A grotto is a fake, fantastic cave –
a word it's difficult to match in rhyme
(like astrolabe). My practice, when I'm stumped,
is – learn from Shakespeare: write blank verse instead!
It seems this architect was never stumped –
or, if he was, he hid it with a joke.

So, park the children and the pram (with babe)
inside this little house that's called a grotto
to see the shells; admire the astrolabe,
the view, the architect's caprice – whose motto,
Cherish the past, adorn the present, while
constructing for the future, makes me smile.

[73]

THE VIEWPOINT

What's special, then, about this Viewpoint? – Not
a lot, unless you count the view, which is
spectacular, of course, like all the rest.
The look-out lacks a name and fails to win
a place or number in the guide-book. Still,
I like it. Stand above the little room
and look around: the hill behind, hotel
beyond the oval swimming-pool, Stone Boat,
and – further – the Observatory Tower,
(another lookout point) lie to your right.
The estuary's in front – and brim-full when
the tide is in: the river reappears
at low-tide, when sands replace the sea.
Across the channel lies another world,
where other people live their different lives.

THE WATER'S EDGE

Although we live on earth, and breathe the air –
this restless wind we sense but never see,
the solid ground that gives stability –
and love the kindly fire that comforts care,
there is no element that can compare
with water to sustain and please. The sea
dances around the land; the rain falls free,
makes deserts flourish, fields grow green and fair.

The steaming kettle and the cube of ice
transform plain water into new delights:
your gin-and-tonic or my cup of tea.
Though just one element may not suffice
for living things (except for fish), our nights
and days are blessed by water, soothed by sea.

THE FLAGPOLE

The land, the language and the people make
the nation – so they say. Portmeirion
suggests it's nature, buildings, and a dream
made real. Or is it empire, anthems, flags?
I pass this flagpole, set beside the sea,
and watch the ensign dancing in the breeze.
I think of Cardiff Arms Park* and the sound
of Welshmen singing for a victory
against the visitors, and hope they win –
unless they're playing England, since I love,
above all others, as they do, the land,
the people, and the language, best of all.

*Now sadly replaced in part by the Millennium Stadium.

THE STONE BOAT

What seas did you once cross in search of land?
What shores approached beneath what harbour bridge?
What grey rocks have you rounded yarely, and
what islands have provided anchorage? ...

... before you reached your final port of call.
and settled – half on land and half at sea –
where this stone boat was built here to recall
the memory of 'Amis Reunis'.*

Boats are like dogs and daughters – dutiful
and dear. They win one's love, then break one's heart –
once lost. We never lose the poignant pull
of memory, when those we love depart.

* The architect's boat was wrecked in a gale on the estuary.

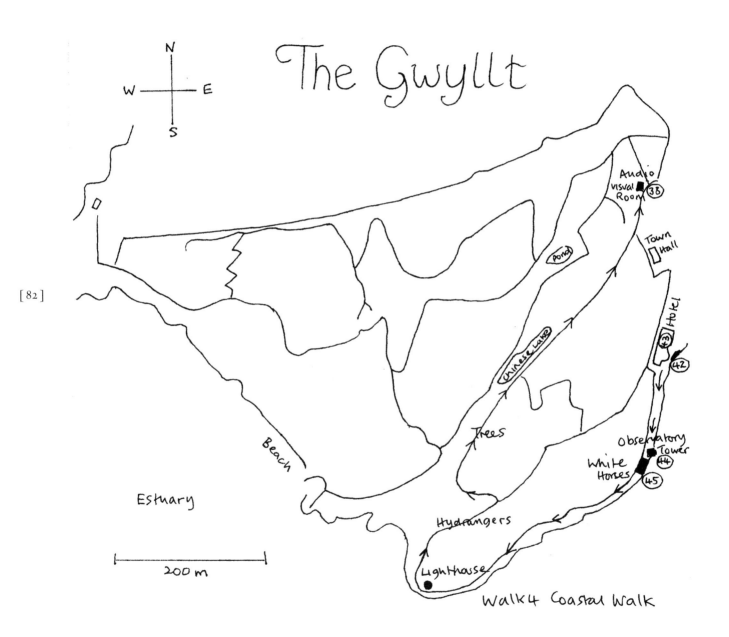

The Gwyllt

N
W E
S

[82]

Audio visual Room 38

Town Hall

Hotel 43 42

Pond

Chinese Lake

Observatory Tower 44

White Horses 45

Trees

Beach

Estuary

Hydrangers

Lighthouse

Walk 4 Coastal Walk

200 m

4. THE COASTAL WALK

THE FOURTH WALK BEGINS WHERE WALK 3 ENDED – at the STONE BOAT [42]. Continue along the coastal path in front of The Hotel [43]: this is the start of Portmeirion's official 'Coastal Walk', which is well sign-posted and easy to follow. Quite soon you reach the OBSERVATORY TOWER [44] and, just beyond it, WHITE HORSES [45]. The path continues along the coast until you reach THE LIGHTHOUSE on the point. Here, the path takes a sharp right-hand bend and starts to ascend into the woods, where you can enjoy the RHODODENDRONS AND HYDRANGEAS and the TREES. Look out for the tree-stumps encrusted with coins. These 'wishing trees' were introduced as recently as 2006, but follow an old Scots tradition dating from the eighteenth century, which held that those who contributed a coin might cure their illness – and those who stole one would catch it! Turn left when you reach the signpost pointing towards the Beach, and then right at the second signpost directing you to the Village and Play Area, before reaching the quiet CHINESE LAKE. The path continues north-eastwards to take you back to the village, where you will find the AUDIO VISUAL ROOM [38].

THE OBSERVATORY TOWER

Only here, only here could you hope to find
such a handsome tower, so attractive a setting
beside the water's edge, beneath the wilderness
they call the Gwyllt – graceful, useless –
with three curiosities: a *camera obscura*,
Nelson's statue and, standing nearby,
a weeping beech. A watchtower without
a watchman, an admiral without an eye, a tree
that weeps for him* (as well it might),
a panoramic darkroom (what a paradox!) –
as strange an assortment of sights as any
I have ever seen. You'll find them only here.

*The tree was actually planted in celebration of the architect's 80th birthday.

White Horses

Here, Thomas Edwards lived, who murdered Mary Jones
two hundred years ago, and hanged (in public) at
Dolgellau. Once a weaver's workshop – also used
for dyeing – here, the star who played The Prisoner
stayed fifty years ago. And you may lodge here now.
The name reminds you that the sea in springtime gales
can rise and drench the cottage. Stay here, if you dare!

I sometimes wonder if man's inhumanity
to man (or woman) is more harmful than the force
of nature and the elemental powers, like storms,
tsunamis, earthquakes, forest fires? The answer is
that we harm nature more than nature injures us.
Like Thomas, who killed Mary, all humanity
is guilty – and must one day pay the penalty.

THE LIGHTHOUSE

Our lives are littered with red flags of warning –
those railway signals, road-signs, traffic lights,
designed to keep us safe – which we are scorning,
intent upon the search for earth's delights.

This lighthouse stands upon the water's edge
to play the guard or guide for passing craft,
but lacks a light. It seems a sacrilege:
an 'unofficial lighthouse' is plain daft,

and irresponsible! And yet – when we,
with all the benefits that gratify
our human lives, live irresponsibly –
why should we grumble, if our mentors lie?

This light-less lighthouse *is* sufficient warning
of pain and penitence tomorrow morning.

[89]

RHODODENDRONS AND HYDRANGEAS

The 'rose-tree' and the 'water-pot'
(I need a native name)
prefer a deeply-shaded spot
(or so the experts claim).

The former likes an acid soil –
which makes the latter blue
(sky-blue, or Cambridge-pale, not royal),
the blooms a bonny view.

The rose-tree's flowers are polychrome,
and large, and bold, and lush.
They decorate the hearth and home,
and make our churches blush.

Both alien invaders – or
welcome settlers here?
An Englishman in Wales, I've more
to answer for – and fear.

TREES

'I see men as trees, walking.' *Mark* viii, 24.

I see trees as women, talking amongst themselves
a secret language of leaves and seasons,
whispering verses by Whitman or Langland,
rhymeless but rhythmical, rocking and swaying
like eastern dancers, all arms and fingers.
kaftan-coloured, clothed in gold-dust:
trees are as common as tables and chairs,
as precious as poetry composed by archangels.

Trees make an alphabet – the ash and the beech,
conifer, damson, and dying elm;
fig-tree, gum-tree, and green-leaved holly.....
Trees provide fruit, firewood and beams
to build a home and help furnish it,
keeping it warm and cooking the meals
of apples and nuts, like nature's housewife.
I see women as trees, working for others.

[93]

THE CHINESE LAKE

Once upon a time he built a house in
China (in Shanghai): the architect must
(I suppose) have come to treasure all those
oriental things – the Buddha, and the
Burmese dancer balanced on a pillar,
or this Chinese lake with Susan's temple
and the Chinese bridge. Portmeirion is
xenophilic: it provides a 'home for
fallen buildings' of all styles and periods –
like the English language, which makes welcome
words like *language, temple, xenophilic ...*
(thousands more) and makes them feel at home here.
Stand and stare at the still lake, the water
and the water-lilies. Let the silence
calm your troubled spirit, nourish kindness,
help us all to learn to smile at strangers.

THE AUDIO VISUAL ROOM

This place is called the Playhouse: who plays here?
The architect *displays* Portmeirion.
His presentation, for both eye and ear,
plays and replays all day to everyone
who steps inside – or none, if no one comes.
Guarding two exits from the village, it's
more modest than most auditoriums –
less spacious too – but mark what it transmits:
unless you listen to his words, you'll miss
the man whose life and work and mindfulness,
whose vision and resolve, created this
success, this triumph. Triumph and success
mean making good things from a good idea:
that's why his great Triumphal Arch stands near.

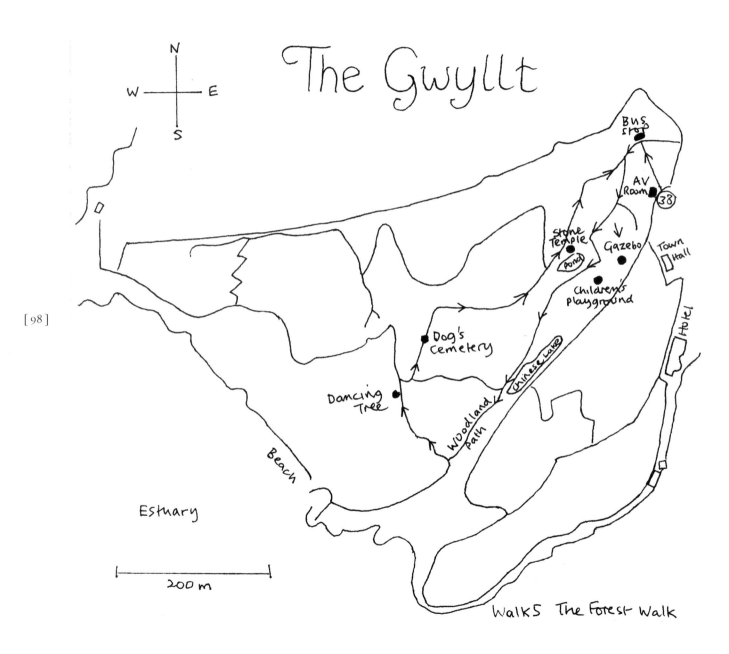

The Gwyllt

N
W   E
S

Bus Stop

A V Room

38

Stone Temple

Pond

Gazebo

Town Hall

Children's Playground

Dog's Cemetery

Chinese Lake

Hotel

Dancing Tree

Woodland path

Beach

Estuary

200 m

Walk 5 The Forest Walk

5. THE FOREST WALK

THE FIFTH WALK STARTS AT THE AV ROOM [33], where Walk 4 ended, and follows the path northwards up the hill. At the top of the hill you come to the BUS STOP. Turn sharp left, and left again, and then take another left turn towards the GAZEBO just before you reach the Old Castell Station sign. Here you will find the remains of the demolished medieval Castell. Then return to the main roadway and continue westwards: THE CHILDREN'S PLAYGROUND appears on the left hand side. On the right you will see the little STONE TEMPLE, which was designed by the architect's daughter, Susan. You might meet the Woodland Train, which follows a route combining parts of both Walks 4 and 5. The path continues, passing the northern edge of the Chinese Lake. Continue straight on in a westerly direction on a footpath, THE WOODLAND PATH, which descends into a hidden valley: turn right at the sign and climb steeply uphill to find THE DANCING TREE and signs to THE DOGS' CEMETERY. Then follow the track and signs to the village in an easterly direction to return to the starting point, where four tracks meet.

THE BUS STOP

I've never seen a bus! I wonder what's
the point of this strange bus-stop, when there's no
bus-service? Possibly, some ancient, slow
(and weird) *celestial omnibus*, with lots

of old Portmeirion celebrities
on board, calls here at night, when no one sees –
blithe spirits, who still haunt these paths and trees,
and that Ghost Garden – they know where it is!

The roll-call of great names who've visited
Portmeirion is endless: Russell, Shaw,
Lloyd George and Wells, Bliss, Walton – and there's more:
the kings and queens and princes, now long dead.

The world's a bus, they say ... Sick of the fuss
and fret of life, some cry for it to stop
and let them off; whilst others wait to hop
aboard, and get a life. There is no bus!

In truth, our lives are empty, meaningless –
Unless we *make* the meaning, *choose* the route,
and *build* the bus. This is our salute
to one who did. We honour his success.

THE GAZEBO

Gazebo means a *viewpoint* or a *belvedere* –
which means a lantern or a turret or
pavilion – which can mean a summerhouse –
which means … you get the point! Portmeirion
is rich in views and rife with viewing sites:
the *Grotto*, the *Observatory Tower* –
and more – the view of Snowdon (or the beach).
A funny word, gazebo, 'I shall gaze' –
sham-Latin, like *videbo*: what I like
about Portmeirion, and names like this,
is both the humour and the vision, shared
with visitors (like you, and me) – in what
was built and what preserved of nature's gift –
of beauty, which the architect, who made
this place, once called 'that strange necessity'.

THE CHILDREN'S PLAYGROUND

All the world's a playground – all the children
champion players: they must one day (sadly)
be transformed to grown-ups, who will lose the
art of play. Portmeirion's a playground,
since the man who made it never ceased to
be a child at heart. This playground is a
playground – in a playground – in a playground!
Watch the children climbing, swinging, sliding;
hear them shouting, laughing, crying; feel the
loss of childhood; learn from happy children.
For a poet claimed 'the child is father
to the man'. Relearn the art of child's play.

THE STONE TEMPLE

It stands above a pool and teases me,
like Keats's Grecian Urn, with questions: who
comes here to worship? which strange deity
inhabits here? what rites are practised? do
the ghosts of dead dogs congregate at night
and dance a foxtrot in the pale moonlight?

'Beauty is truth, truth beauty.' That
is all we know on earth – and all we need.
Portmeirion provides a habitat
for both, presenting Clough's persuasive creed
of architecture (concrete poetry)
that beauty is a 'strange necessity'.

I feel the frozen music, as I stand
beside the quiet pool. I hear his voice.
'I made a home for fallen buildings, planned
a place to make perceptive eyes rejoice.
You want a church? Walk in the woods alone
and find this little temple built of stone.'

The Woodland Path

They made a path through woods
beside the estuary of Afon Dwyryd.
Geese honked. The leaves were falling in the rain.
They cut the brushwood back, levelled the ground,
wrestled with thorns and bramble-bushes. Then,
scouting ahead through undergrowth to mark
the line, they found that they were following
some faint deer-tracks. I guess I ought to say:
    they found a path through woods.

They found a path through woods
beside the estuary of Afon Dwyryd.
I like the way it swerves down to the water,
then climbs a little hill to open ground.
They made a bridge across a streamlet – more
for show, than use. – I see it's not our words,
or thoughts, or feelings, that define us. But
our actions do. Perhaps I should have said:
    our path through life makes us.

THE DANCING TREE

So – is this 'dancing tree' a tree that really dances?
Or just another tree that children dance around?
Although I'd dearly like to see the former, chances
are these firm roots, strong trunk, have never left the ground.

A maple might provide a ribboned maypole, but
you shouldn't try to tango by a mango, or
perform the hokey-cokey near a coconut.
Trees never dance: their role's to make the ballroom floor!

And yet, to tell the truth, I sometimes wish they did.
Just think – a dancing tree! Idly, I turn my glance
from roots and trunk towards the branches where, amid
the gentle breeze and sunlight, the leaves seem to dance.

THE DOGS' CEMETERY

I have fallen in love with those old dogs' names:
La Belle and Arabella, Nelson, Prince ...
These modest stones and kindly words convince
the visitor that Roger, Sam and James,
Flora and Jess are not forgotten. Fame's
a prize a dog may earn! These dogs, long since
deceased, are still remembered here, with hints
of happy days, shared walks and madcap games.

Trixie and Topsy, Henrietta, Ted,
Roger and Pepys and Patch proved faithful friends.
They loved, were loved – and met their several ends.
Their lives were mourned. These monuments endear
us to these animals. When I am dead,
scatter a spoonful of my ashes here.

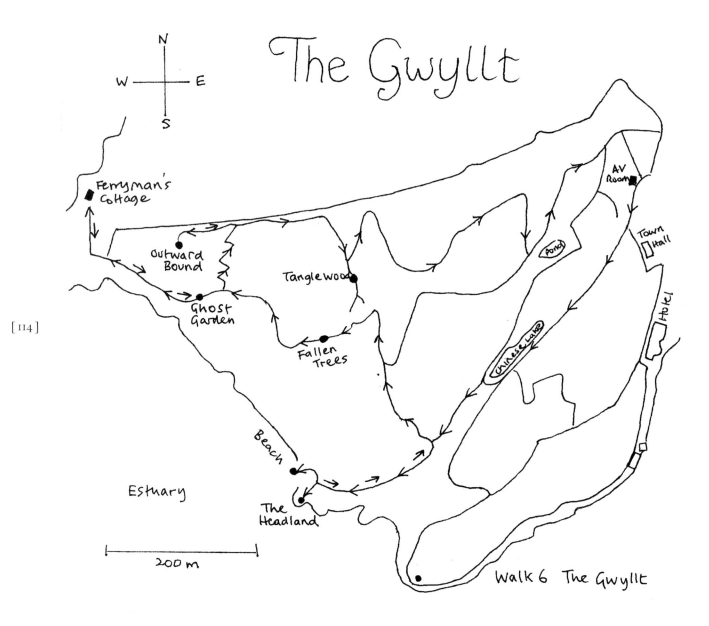

The Gwyllt

N
W E
S

Ferryman's Cottage

Outward Bound

Ghost Garden

Tanglewood

Fallen Trees

Beach

Estuary

The Headland

Chinese Lake

Pond

A.V. Room

Town Hall

Hotel

200 m

Walk 6 The Gwyllt

6. THE GWYLLT

THE GWYLLT IS THE WILDERNESS OF TREES AND SHRUBS BEYOND THE FOREST WALK (Walk 5). Start by taking the route from the AV Room along which you returned to the village at the end of Walk 4, passing the Chinese Lake (on your right), and then follow signs, which take you past THE HEADLAND to THE BEACH. You can walk on the beach at low tide, but take care once the tide turns. Now, return the way you came to find a path branching left, with FALLEN TREES: take this and follow the signs to THE GHOST GARDEN. Then, follow the path that leads westwards as far as you can go to find THE FERRYMAN'S COTTAGE. Return the way you came through the Ghost Garden, until you find a path on the left that zigzags steeply up the hill. Follow it and turn left at the top to reach a look-out point called Bone's View. There is a comfortable bench, where you can enjoy the outlook that we call OUTWARD BOUND. Return eastwards towards Portmeirion, passing the zigzag path; then turn right at the next turning to find TANGLEWOOD. Now go back to the top of the hill, turn right (eastwards), returning to the village by one of several paths. We recommend the one highlighted below.

THE OUTLOOK FROM THE HEADLAND

Look out across the unfathomable sea:
life's voyage and our futures are unknown,
unknowable – we journey on alone.
The little craft has cleared the estuary,
rounded the point, and reached the open sea –
and now those mariners are on their own.

We choose between the ocean and the land –
the harbour, hamlet, hills beyond – about
a mile or two across the sound. No doubt,
we'd feel at home there. On the other hand,
the ocean offers sights as yet unscanned.
But, if you choose the open sea, look out!

THE BEACH

> The high tide licks the rocks
> and soaks the base of the steep cliff that guards
> the Afon Dwyryd estuary, and keeps
> Portmeirion secure against the sea.
> The water laps the rocks.
>
> I turn towards the land:
> The Gwyllt, a labyrinth of trees and paths
> and caves, and further to the north, the peaks
> of Snowdon and the mountains of north Wales.
> I look across the land.
>
> But when I turn again,
> the tide has turned. The sands appear and spread.
> The sea recedes. Children are splashing in
> the shallow water draining down the beach.
> Until it turns again.
>
> We never see the point
> of turn of tides, nor yet of human life,
> which soon or late must run into the sand,
> nor when that irreversible low tide
> slackens. We miss the point.

Fallen Trees

Some trees survive for centuries. Like tortoises,
or pyramids, or patriarchs, their lives persist
through generations of mere mortal beings. Is
this why I feel so sad when trees cease to exist?

These fallen trees remind me of mortality.
Methuselah met death at last; the Sphynx that smiles
still sinks beneath the sands of time – if gradually;
those giant turtles die. Grim death brooks no denials.

All flesh is grass. Dead trees seem monstrous haystalks mown
by time's inevitable harvest, which will reap
all living things, all artefacts, all art, we've known
and loved. Not books, nor buildings, you nor I, will keep.

All creatures, all creations, reach their final bed,
and die, one day. Still firm, still mighty, fallen trees
seem more like actors resting than things really dead.
I hope that, when I fall, I feel at rest – like these.

The Ghost Garden

So, where's the ghost? you ask, and where's the garden?
Like beauty in the eyes of the beholder,
ghosts are imaginary! We must pardon
the fancy of Portmeirion's freeholder.
Gardens are real enough: this is just woodland –
well-managed woodland, maybe, but it's fruitless,
flower-free, not because it isn't good land.
Seeds sown in soil like this would not be rootless.
So, what's the point of pointing the wood-walkers
towards a garden (or a ghost) that's not there?
I guess – to prompt the thinkers and the talkers.
Ghost-garden? Get the idea! *Now*, you've got there.
    Portmeirion's a double-faced creation:
    figment *and* fillip of imagination.

[123]

THE FERRYMAN'S COTTAGE

As far as one can go to be alone
on this estate – neglected, overgrown,
this cottage by the sea, all on its own,
half-hidden in the steep hill's side, unknown

to all, save walkers in the wilderness
who, asked to go that extra mile say *yes* –
regardless of the dangers or distress –
awaits destruction or reprieve: you guess!

Turquoise or pink? They'll surely keep the roof
of slates and low-set windows, weatherproof
and Welsh, traditional as warp and woof,
not some Portmeirion *trompe l'oeil* spoof.

Who was the ferryman? What was his life,
who launched his little boat into the strife
of wind and water, where sunk rocks are rife?
Did he have children and a patient wife?

This cottage was a place of solitude,
where shy musicians played unheard, unviewed,
and artists painted, poets came to brood –
and artists' models sunbathed in the nude!

OUTWARD BOUND

θάλαττα, θάλαττα ('The sea! The sea!'), Xenophon, *The Anabasis*

We drop through waterfalls down to an ocean
of sunlight and air. Suddenly grateful
for faces and voices, we feed upon raindrops
of milk and attention, immersed in rivers
of sleep and love, starting life's journeys
fellowed by water – a friend that proves lasting.

Playing with water yields pleasures lasting
a lifetime: watching waves in the ocean
from perilous shores, or ships on their journeys;
swimming or sailing; the sea makes us grateful.
Water's our playmate in pools and rivers,
or gardens nourished by glistening raindrops.

Water works for us too: wells fed by raindrops,
kettles and cisterns – the simple everlasting
water-cycle: seas, clouds, rivers
turning mill-wheels as they marathon to the ocean;
hydro-electric heating at home; we are grateful
for canals and sea-lanes providing safe journeys.

The four elements are never absent from our journeys
through life – fire, earth, air and raindrops.
One and all seem miraculous. Each makes us grateful.
But water is wizardry outlasting
familiarity, a single drip or the deepest ocean.
We're distracted by streams, astonished by rivers.

Water's a friend – but also a foe: rivers
may flood, and ships founder on journeys
amidst menacing mountains of ocean.
Such damage and destruction from delicate raindrops!
Water wrecks, and renews – for nothing is lasting:
a natural wonder of the world. Be grateful

for the bewildering metamorphoses of water – grateful
for snowfalls and icebergs, salmon-filled rivers,
storm-clouds and mist on the mountains lasting
day-long, steam power for Stephenson's journeys,
hot sulphur springs, sparkling raindrops,
still tarns feeding the eternal ocean.

Learn to be grateful on life's journeys
for the mysteries of rivers and the magic of raindrops,
as you seek lasting solace in the ocean.

[127]

TANGLEWOOD

This Tanglewood provides a wall
repelling errant passers-by,
like us: is that the point of all
   this Tanglewood?

These twisted branches catch the eye.
Portmeirion's appeal won't pall,
its charm can't fade, until we die.

In summer, flowers *en masse* enthral
the memory and senses. I
imagine *that* is why they call
   this 'Tanglewood'.

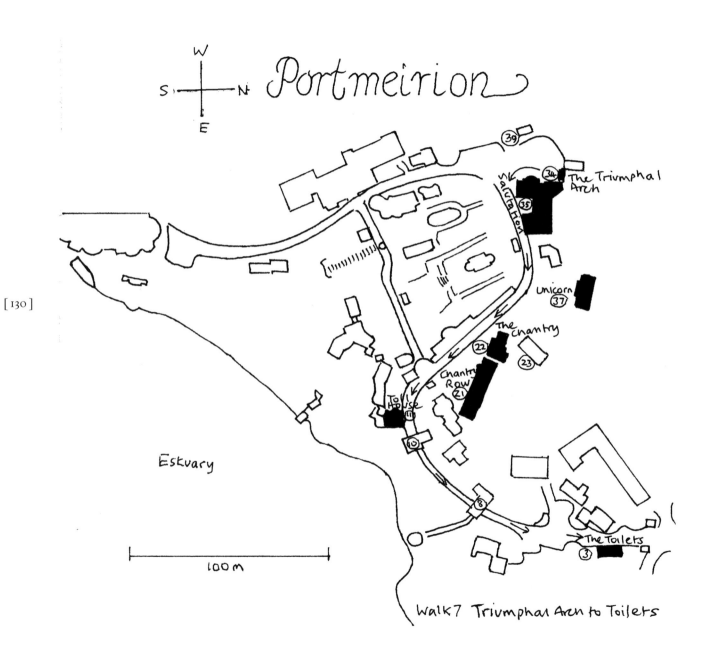

Portmeirion

W · S · N · E

[130]

The Triumphal Arch

Salutation

Unicorn 37

The Chantry
22
23

Chantry Row 21

Toll House

Estuary

100m

Walk 7 Triumphal Arch to Toilets

The Toilets
3

7. THE TRIUMPHAL ARCH TO THE CAR PARK

THE LAST WALK STARTS AT THE TRIUMPHAL ARCH [34], near the AV Room [39], and follows the road back up the hill towards the entrance to (and exit from) Portmeirion. You will find SALUTATION [35] on the left almost at once. UNICORN [37] is also on your left, set back from the road, a little further on. The road swings to the right and you soon reach THE CHANTRY [22] – behind it is The Villa Winch [23] – and CHANTRY ROW [21]. The road now begins to bend to the left: THE TOLL HOUSE [11] is on the right. Continue up the hill, passing beneath Bridge House [10] and Gate House [8] once more – Chantry Lodge [4] and Portmeirion's Offices [5] are on the left – to find THE TOILETS [3] on the right just in front of The Tollgate [1] and exit.

THE TRIUMPHAL ARCH

Look at this lovely picture of the Arch
that Susan asked her father to design
to help protect the village from the march
of time and traffic-menace, which combine

to spoil the centres of most city-scapes,
where planners and pedestrians alike
cower before the motor-car – which rapes
our streets. I love this arch, and like

the way it hides the service-road which takes
the traffic round the back – a neat device
which still permits deliveries, yet makes
Portmeirion this car-free Paradise.

This pale rococo Arch provides a home
for an old model for a Caryatid
beneath the angled top – now more a dome –
the architect designed. Nothing he did

lacked purpose, nothing failed to satisfy
'that strange necessity' called beauty. This
eclectic architecture pleases my
desire for humour, use – and loveliness.

[133]

SALUTATION

One of the four old buildings that predate
Portmeirion, this stable-block has been
transformed into a café or canteen,
and then a shop where visitors who wait
for tea can buy the cup! The roof (of slate)
and twisted chimneys also can be seen
above The Mermaid and Hotel. Between
the old and new – this style's appropriate.

The architect has understood good style
requires a sensitivity to what
was there before – the sea and woods and skies,
and these four buildings. Innovation, while
it must not be resisted, yet should not
be impolite, or make us hide our eyes.

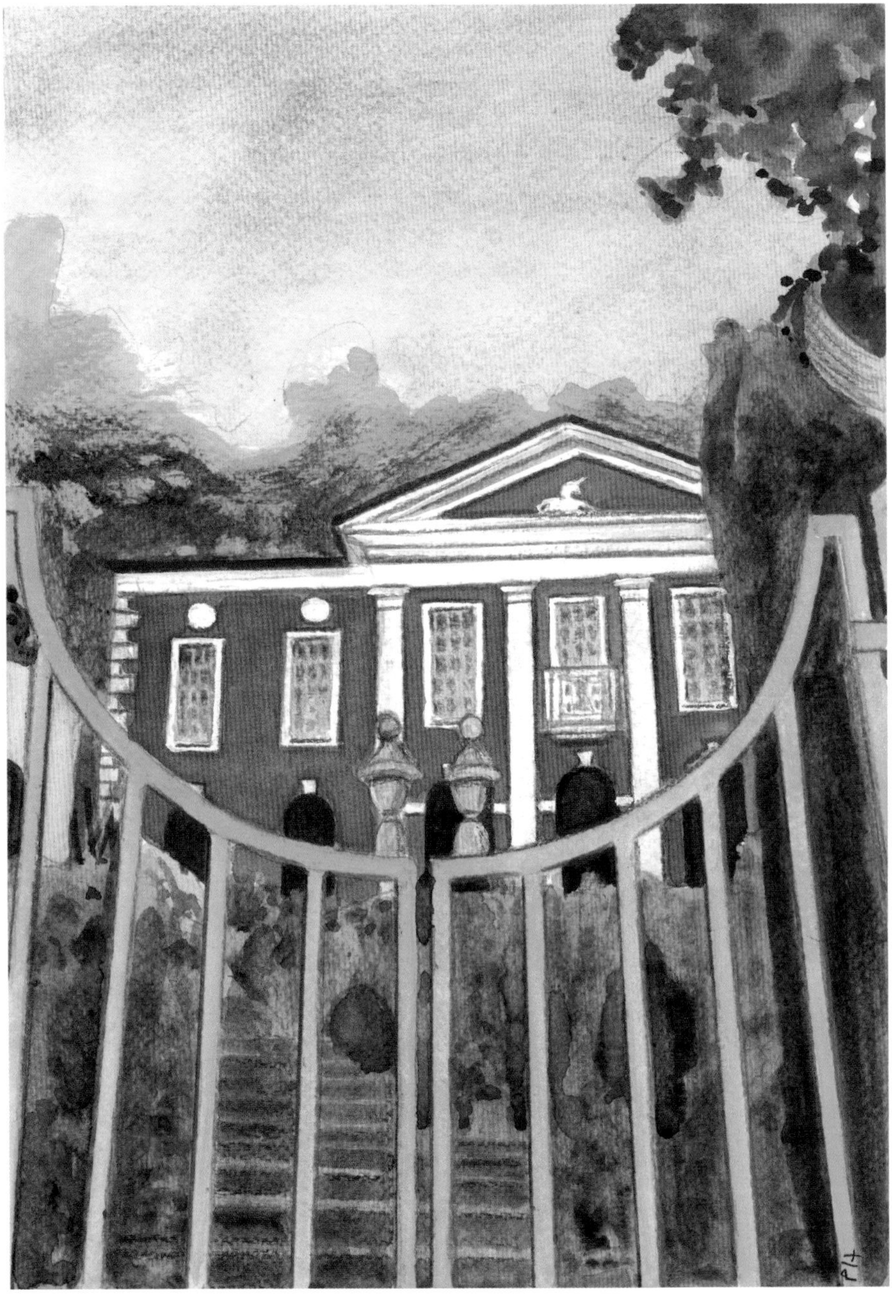

UNICORN

This 'mini-Chatsworth' was the architect's
favourite building, so it's said. Its style
is Classical, a Georgian pastiche –
provided that you view it from the front!

Who wanders round the other side, detects
deception. What you see will make you smile –
a flat-roofed bungalow! The nouveau riche
might like it: purists find it an affront.

Experience and education – each affects
our taste. We find things worthy or worthwhile,
if they're familiar. Would I could unleash
the chains of use and habit, and confront

the new with a fresh vision that respects
a thing for what it is, and reconcile
myself to it – not seek a mental niche
to place it in, then shun it with a grunt.

THE CHANTRY

Built on the highest point above the road
and village green, this house provides for eight
to sleep. It boasts three bathrooms, an ornate
lantern or cupola: a fine abode –
for any poet who would pen an ode,
or any artist seeking to create
a picture of the view across the strait –
windowed and chimney-ed, tiled and studio-ed.
(And yet Augustus John once turned it down!)
The name suggests a chapel and the Mass
sung by some lonely monk in sable gown.
The truth's more trivial and trite, alas!
The architect just liked the name. It's true!
He was an artist – and a poet, too.

CHANTRY ROW

Like so much seen here at Portmeirion,
this Chantry Row is not quite what it seems –
a terrace of four painted cottages
surmounted by an onion dome. The dome
(designed to hide the chimney) is just half
a dome on half a turret, and the space
inside the Row provides two suites of rooms,
not four, each grand enough to house a prince.
This is no peasant terrace for the poor
poet or artist (you and me?) – the ones
who work in words and colours to create
something they hope might be more than it seems.

[141]

THE TOLL HOUSE

'Shamelessly picturesque' he called this place –
beside the 'elegant formality'
he gave its neighbour, Bridge House: one has grace,
the other strangeness. Visitors may see
the over-sailing upper storeys and
the rugged weather-boarding, painted black,
in Scandinavian style. This house was planned
to mark the entrance: now, set so far back,
the name seems inappropriate. It shows
you how Portmeirion has grown and spread
since 1925. Examine those
embellishments – St. Peter, dressed in red,
the sheep Clough's daughter (Susan) made, the signs
and plaques presenting picturesque designs.

The Toilets

Good architects inspire and comfort us:
so William Butterfield gave chimneys to
his college chapel – for he argued thus:
'The students will have souls – and bodies too'.

This building's where the tourist finds relief.
These rest-rooms serve the usual offices.
Whether your visit be prolonged, or brief,
study the benches and the canopies.

Here's a convenience designed to please
the visitor, whose mind's on lower things.
Admire the colours, as you take your ease,
the neat proportions and the furnishings.

You should not shun the sewer or the sluice
where form embraces function, beauty use.

ENVOI

Portmeirion's like Marmite: love or hate
is what the viewer feels, and very few
then change their minds. I wonder who
hates it? What's not to like! Articulate
critics complain that it's *contrived*. All great
art is! A pastry and a pretty view
give pleasure: who wants more? For those who do,
this place will move, inspire and elevate.

True, happiness is found in deeper wells
than pleasure – which the company of friends
and family, and culture, yield. It dwells
in service, freely given, making or
achieving something worthy... When life ends
we'll find, as Clough did, that's what life was for.

ACKNOWLEDGEMENTS

We want to take this opportunity to thank Robin Llywelyn and Meurig Jones, of Portmeirion Ltd, for their interest in this project, comments and generous support.